A GRAPHOLOGY STUDENT'S WORKBOOK

A Workbook for Group Instruction or Self Study
by Ruth Gardner

Second Edition 1975
LLEWELLYN PUBLICATIONS
P.O. Box 3383, St. Paul, MN 55165
U.S.A.

ISBN 0-87542-250-0
First Edition 1973
Second Edition 1975

Publisher: LLEWELLYN PUBLICATIONS, St. Paul, Minn.

Printed in the United States of America

Dedicated to

Prince Bokovoy, Jr.

Whose enthusiasm and thirst for
knowledge proved so very infectious

TABLE OF CONTENTS

PREFACE TO SECOND EDITION

A consistent desire by searching persons, for information concerning the self and how that self relates to the world, has brought this book to a second printing. There have been some changes made in various areas of the book and in particular in the chapter on spacing. A few items have been deleted and a few added in the interest of clarity but it remains essentially the same book.

It is the author's eager desire that whoever chooses to use this book as one of the means to increase his knowledge of the self should find the information to help make that possible.

PREFACE

Current interest in increasing one's self-awareness has caused many people to turn their attention to the science of graphology. While there is a fair amount of resource material, there is a dearth of beginning or simple reference material which could be used by students to develop a foundation upon which to build. There seems also to be a need for a resource which could be used as a personal reference; one that would permit the student to add information as it is acquired. A compilation of the various forms given letters, and a description of the characteristics thought to be indicated by each, is included to add to the value of the book as a reference.

Graphologists agree that it is imperative for students of graphology to perceive this science as more than a "parlor game" and to strive to develop self-awareness as they learn to analyze others' handwriting. For these reasons, readers will find suggestions for analyzing their own emotional reactions, to forming various strokes.

Finally, it is hoped that this book will help those striving to learn more about themselves in a manner that is fun, interesting and not necessarily complicated.

I. INTRODUCTION

One of the definitions of graphology describes it as a study and scientific analysis of handwriting or the art of interpreting character and personality from diagnostic peculiarities of handwriting. This work will dwell on and attempt to cover for the beginning student of Graphology the basic factors of this definition.

Before beginning the study of Graphology, every student should be aware of some of the things Graphology cannot tell the analyst about the writer. First and foremost, it cannot foretell the future. Many people equate Graphology with some kind of extra sensory perception or clairvoyance. It is neither of these. As mentioned before, it is a scientific study. A graphologist may predict a writer's reaction to various situations, but this is not predicting the future. A second factor, which is usually not even attempted by the analyst, is the exact age of the writer. One can often perceive the very old and the very young but at times even this is difficult. Another factor some analysts will guess at but can never be positive of is the sex of the writer. Certain traits are often assigned by our social values as belonging to the male or female but especially with the recent trend toward changing many of these values, these traits in many cases prove invalid. A thorough analyst will require knowledge of age and sex before beginning an analysis if at all possible.

It seems important to insert a few words of caution in the process of disseminating the information which is to follow. Perhaps the most important of these is that Graphology is a tool, and only a tool, and should be used along with other means to obtain an accurate profile. This is followed in importance by the fact that every trait is a clue and only a clue and must be evaluated together with other traits and every trait is influenced by every other trait. In addition, the analyst must remember that the great majority of traits possess both a positive and a negative aspect and all must be evaluated by considering all contributing factors.

The uses for a graphological interpretation are many and varied. Perhaps the most common is for vocational counseling or determining position adaptability. A capable graphologist operating as a consultant in a personnel department often saves a business time and money by assisting in the assignment of employees to a position where they will be most productive and content.

Premarital compatibility evaluations are also a function of Graphology and are used extensively in some areas. Information concerning a beloved's shortcomings might not discourage an impending marriage but would probably better prepare those involved for forthcoming problems through awareness.

Detecting physical abnormalities through an examination by a knowledgeable graphologist is often helpful information for a variety of reasons. Due to the fact that this is a specialized field, it will not be covered in this work but is available in more advanced writings. However, it would be well to mention Alfred Knafer, a pioneer in cancer diagnosis through Graphology. He has become a well known expert in this field because of his extreme accuracy.

The final application which will be mentioned is the use of Graphology in the therapy for those who desire or need changes in attitudes and habits. Paul de Sainte Colombe and his wife, Kathi, have dedicated much of their lives to this end. *Pen and Pencil Therapy* or *Grapho-Therapeutics* written by Mr. de Sainte Colombe covers this subject thoroughly and interestingly.

When an individual requests an analysis there are several simple rules the analyst will probably find helpful in guiding the writer's preparation of the sample:
1. Use unlined paper, at least six inches by nine inches and preferably larger; never a napkin, a grocery list, post card or anything similar.
2. Have the writer use his usual pen, fountain or ballpoint—not a pencil.
3. Request a minimum of one hundred words; more if a deeper analysis is desired.
4. Discourage the writer from copying from a paper or book or from writing poetry.

After receiving the sample the analyst should remember that each trait is a clue and only a clue, an occasional sign may mean an occasional trait and a frequent sign probably means a frequent trait.

A good beginning appears to be the bottom of the sample since the writer may be self-conscious in his beginning and is quite likely to forget this as he proceeds. Recent letters can very often be used as adequate samples.

Always remember a disciplined Graphologist does not jump to conclusions as a result of a few clues but evaluates the entire sample carefully, relying on more than one factor before making a judgment.

There are many areas in Graphology which will not be covered in this work as they are entire fields by themselves. Some of these areas include signatures, doodles and medical analysis. As the analyst advances in knowledge and skill there are many books available on these more advanced areas.

The transparencies in the center of this book are removable and used for assisting the analyst in calculating the degrees of various factors. The individual transparencies will be discussed in each particular section relating to them.

There are also spaces left in each section for the new analyst to write in additional information or attach meaningful samples for later reference.

An interesting fact which the reader will soon discover is the obviousness of the meanings. A student could probably logically arrive at many if not all of the facts which will be dealt with on the following pages, if there were time, interest and dedication available. A method which many Graphologists use to investigate an unknown trait or stroke is trying to use the same movement with their hand which the writer did when making the original. This effort may, with practice, help lead the searcher to the answer.

It seems important to insert a few words concerning signatures. An individual's signature displays to the reader the manner which the writer desires to have the reader interpret his or her personality, so it cannot be used as a basis for a *true* personality analysis. In some cases the signature and the body of the writing may indicate the same traits, but this is not always true.

ZONES

Three zones are used in writing analysis and the approximate position on paper often corresponds to the area involved in the writer's body.

For instance, a high reaching upper zone may signify a reaching mind, whereas a large full lower zone may imply interest in sex or material possessions.

Consider how you, the reader, feel when making certain types of strokes. Check your writing when a rare mood affects you or when a new and changing experience has occurred. Practice being aware of your own feelings and how they are expressed on paper. Remember an emphasis in one zone must detract from the other two and very rarely are all three zones consistantly balanced.

II. ZONES

UPPER	intellectual or abstract
MIDDLE	daily action or tangible
LOWER	desire and drives or biological

Middle zone

acemnoxsuvuxz

This middle zone contains all of the single zone or unizonal letters and parts of all of the other letters. It is often called the area of the visible personality and the unimaginative area. Various extremes in this zone indicate extremes or marked interest in the areas of:
  social relationships
  mundane, everyday parts of life
  the here and now
  the conscious action mind
  habits and behavior patterns
  daily goals
  tangible aspects of life

Middle zone accentuated at the expense of other zones indicates a particular interest in social relationships and conscious action at the expense of the material drives and desires and the intellectual aspects of life.

The writer is often said to be immature or insecure because of this imbalance. Frequently, the accentuation appears in the writing of young people in the process of maturing. They need to be particularly conscious of daily happenings and social relationships to identify with the process of maturing.

of moss

lined with

walk

such an easy

period in history

name that will

must have i

Upper zone

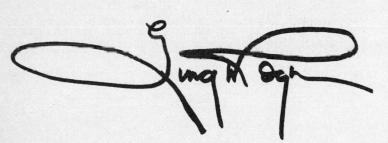

A small deaccentuated middle zone may indicate concentration in one of the other zones, probably at the expense of their daily life. It is probable that they are careless of the impressions they make and give no attention to expressing their own emotional needs.

This zone contains the two zone, or bizonal, letters which reach up from the middle zone, the i dots, t bars, the letter f which covers all three zones, called trizonal, and part of all of the capital letters. Various extremes in this zone indicate departure from the ordinary in intangible and intellectual fields such as:

> science
> politics
> spirituality
> abstractness
> philosophy
> imagination
> creativity
> fantasy

happy to comply

The large full upper loops divulge a thoughtful person, probably with imagination and creativity.

The more flourished or enlarged or twirled the more extreme the imagination and the more indicative of fantasy (daydreams).

6

pulled
sent along
end and

A decreased size or unbalanced writing at the expense of this zone would indicate a lack of attention or consideration of the intellectual aspects.

absolutely no furniture except

Lets see what tomorrow

If this zone has some originality and expressiveness, a fairly narrow, high, upper zone might indicate caution in thought but definite interest in the thought and/or abstract area.

if all the

A narrow upper zone reveals lack of imagination or creative thought if there is no originality or creativity shown elsewhere.

Lower zone

The lower zone contains all bizonal letters or those which reach down into it from the middle zone, and also part of the letter f, the only trizonal letter. Extremes in lower-zone length may indicate extent of interest in biological drives and desires; extremes in pressure, the intensity of those desires; in slant, the frequency of the need; and in width, the amount of thought and/or speech involved. The lower zone is considered the area of the id or subconscious world and includes interests in:
  physical expenditures
  sex and love

sports and adventures
instincts and drives
material interests,
       money and belongings

giant

your quite young

Full (long and wide) lower loops denote an active imagination. Someone "on display", perhaps an actor or athlete and certainly a gregarious being. A need to hang on to money is also indicated by this sort of full finished loop, particularly the y.

I may go

Exaggeration of lower loops often shows an interest in the instinctive world, probably more than average.

my py my

say of finding

Unusual lower loop formation denotes eccentricity or repression in the field of drives and desires, often in sex. Frequent unusual loops are often said to reveal unusual lovers.

very enjoyable

vacation with

Very long lower loops show much involvement, if tangled into the lower line, obviously overinvolvement.

confusion

Angular bottom or lower loop formations indicates uncompromising resentment, hostility and perhaps difficulty in sexual gratification.

ya going my

carrying

rarely

ready and

again. O

other soft

or grass

by

Unclosed loops show frustration in the instinctive, (money or sex) matters.

No loops whatsoever probably represent materialistic and sexual repression. Individuals often omit loops if the letter is the last in a word but usually loops can be found in loop letters falling in the center of the word. A firm single stroke down is also a sign of firmness, of supervisory ability.

Very short lower loops show unimportance of basic drives, of materialism. There are probably concentrations in one of the other zones.

LINE AND LETTER LEANINGS

Line slant probably denotes pessimism versus optimism better than any other factor. Check your own writing when feeling depressed or discouraged. Unless you have a great deal of control the lines will probably descend. Do you feel loved, sunny, accomplished? Chances are pretty good that your writing ascends at a time like this. These climbing or falling tendencies may be temporary or they can be an announcement of your general feelings toward and about life.

Letter slant may be interpreted in several ways but perhaps the most common has to do with the writer's emotional direction and degree of emotional control. As mentioned before, the obvious is usually the answer. The writer whose writing leans forward does just that emotionally. A right slanted writer leans toward friendships and the future while a left slanted one is leaning back to the past and away from people. The left slanted may isolate themselves more but by this very act may tend to be more creative. Their lives probably aren't so intertwined with other individuals and there is more time and energy for creativity to surface.

Again, check your own degree of slant during an emotional period, during stressful intervals and at times of uninvolvement; consider why you write as you do.

III. LINE AND LETTER LEANINGS

Line leaning or line slant

The analyst may wish to use Transparency No. 1 in assisting in determining the line leaning. Place the edge of the transparency on the corresponding edge of the sample and observe the direction of the line through the transparency.

The direction of the line may be dependent on a temporary condition such as mental state or physical condition. In order to take account of this factor for an accurate analysis the analyst needs several different samples written at different times.

An aid to deciding the actual slant of the line if this is difficult to ascertain is to turn the sample and look at it from the side, rather than in the usual reading position.

When the base line of the writing slants up to the right the following are indicated:
optimism
faith in the future
feeling of being loved
excitement
joy

When the base line slants down to the right:
pessimism
dispirited
fatigued
discouraged
depressed

All well here. The pace hasn't slowed for January tho. Bud was assigned ten days vacation end of January. Among other things had hoped to get into the attic

the house was too

Anyhow, this is good I play the guitar.

And so today we see the out come is not

is like the best that there is

Baseline parallel to top and bottom of page:
   reliability
   even temper
   control of emotions
   reasoning rules
   unwavering resolution
   often uninteresting or dull

Baseline forms a definite arc:
   Writer begins project or interest with enthusiasm and optimism but tires of it and gives up, probably doesn't finish a lot of the projects which are started.

Baseline forms a dish or concave:
   Writer is a slow starter without a lot of confidence or purpose, perhaps due to bad breaks or health, but as project progresses, writer will overcome much of beginning negativism and complete the project or become optimistic about the outcome.

Constant baseline but descending words indicate a fight against depression and a lack of self-confidence. These writers need encouragement and do well if encouraged.

Constant baseline, but words ascending, reveal the writer has enthusiasm and probably an over-optimistic view toward life. It also denotes an absence of continued stamina.

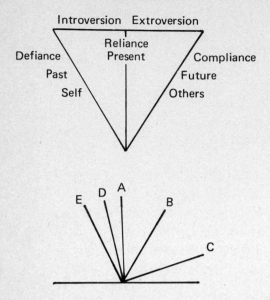

In addition to the diagrams on the left, the analyst may wish to use Transparency No. 2, which is found in the center of this book to assist in deciding the degree of letter slant. The capital letters A B C D E are used on the diagram as well as the transparency to help the analyst in organizing this factor.

The slant of the letters indicate the connection between the writer's inner and outer world. It is the writer's reaction to environmental factors. About 77 percent of the people who write do so with a right slant, 15 percent use a left slant and the remaining 8 percent write vertically.

Now we know the
and the people

please put

A. Vertical slant:
    head controls heart
    matter of fact personality
    ability to keep emotions in control in crises
    independent emotional nature
    orientated to work well alone
    lack of spontaneity

B. Moderate Right slant
    ability to express opinions
    confidence in convictions
    freedom of thought
    extroversion

although he

into the swing of things

very writing

the middle
fatter than if
Monday

walking

must stay off

future orientation
demonstrative and expressive
easily influenced
affectionate and kind
impulsive to a minor degree

C. Extreme Right slant:
   lack of self control
   impulsiveness
   unrestrained
   intense, involved and individual
   expressiveness
   supersensitivity (possibly radical)
   dependence on others
   little resistance to impressions
   low frustration tolerance (violent)

D. Moderate Left slant:
   reflectiveness
   independence
   choosiness about color, designs, wording,
   materials, all things concerning self such as
   clothes, car and especially friends.
   objectiveness
   lack of sympathy
   difficulty in expressing emotions
   self-containment
   possible repression and inhibition
   difficulty in adaptation
   rejection of environment

E. Extreme Left slant:
   repressed childhood
   possible rejection by parents
   fear of the future
   evading reality

apprehensiveness about intimate social
relationships
disillusionment and defiance
self defending

F. Irregular slant:
extreme sensitivity
moodiness
unpredictability
versatility
ambivalence

Emotional
exchange

SIZE

There are many variations and combinations of the size of a letter and each has its own meaning. For reasons of simplicity and space this work will attempt to cover only the main ones which are: tall, small, broad and narrow. The various combinations should be, in most cases, apparent. Being aware of the amount of space you, as an individual, require can help you to understand the traits which the size of your writing contributes to your personality.

IV. SIZE

The size of the writing usually indicates the size the writer claims among other people. It is a measure of self-esteem. If all unizonal letters are less than two millimeters the writing is considered small, if over three millimeters, the writing is tall or large. The bizonal letters should be once again the size of the unizonal ones. Transparencies No. 4 and No. 5 may be used, if desired, to help ascertain the writing size.

I hope this will cover the I'm going because I'm and not

Tall writing indicates:
    importance of approval to the writer
    ambition
    observation of things in general, not in detail
    lack of objectivity
    lack of consideration
    lack of modesty
    lack of tact
    self satisfaction

ticking the time me which he really eddy game ewe too many peanuts

Small writing indicates:
    writer looks at life through a microscope
    analytical nature (takes things apart)
    modesty and reserve
    ability to concentrate
    unconcern of own image
    resourcefulness
    thriftiness
    lack of self confidence
    resignation

to write distinctly
slowly— to write
to use a pen
this one has.

obedience
accurate individual
observant
conservativeness concerning money and time

Width of the writing is usually expected to denote the amount of living space or elbow room the writer needs or demands.

the windows—
blue slacks

Off
This went
number two
excitement,

telephone the
so that I'll
I've set out

Broad or Wide writing implies:
   desire for travel
   need to spend on self
   fantasizing nature
   boastful nature
   self assurance
   egotism
   indescretion
   pride
   lack of concentration
   tolerance
   lack of discipline and tact
   natural approach
   frankness
   friendliness

there were few people who could believe in the federal Government

away. [illegible] is enjoy. I en, went to together

Narrow writing shows:
    restriction
    conservatism
    inhibition
    self discipline
    economical nature
    concentration ability
    distrustful nature
    socially passive individual

irregular the more of the U.S. in flocks

Tall unizonal letters indicate:
    desire for greatness
    hero worship
    fondness for food
    eccentricity

of the clock paid)

Irregular letter size:
    moodiness
    vivaciousness
    quick temper
    excitable

Capital letter size

Tall and narrow:
  shyness and pride
  pretention
  coolness

Tall and exaggerated:
  imagination
  ambition
  artistic talent
  braggart
  compensation for inferiority complex

Tapering down to the right:
  diplomacy
  condescension
  patronizing attitude

Tapering up to the right:
  outward confidence but inner subordination
  immaturity and childishness
  self-consciousness

Unnecessary caps within sentences:
  ostentation

PRESSURE

A feeling of dominance or intensity may produce a different type of pressure than one of sympathy or carefulness. However, a writer will most usually use a consistant form of pressure. As mentioned before, it is a learning experience to make yourself aware of the pressure you use and the feelings you have to go with this pressure.

V. PRESSURE

Pressure is the graphologist's measure of the writer's vitality, intensity and determination. It is not a conscious trait and is usually not done with the writer's awareness. Pressure shows the urge or lack of urge of the writer's personality.

Heavy pressure can be better felt, perhaps, than seen. In the days of ball-point pens, the depth of the impression on the back of the paper is a measure of heavy pressure. Felt tip pens can also indicate heavy pressure, particularly if the images on the paper are wide and spread out.

A writer with heavy pressure indicates a deeply intense personality, a strong vitality and probably one with strong determination. These writers soak up emotional experiences and retain the impression made by these experiences for long periods of time.

Heavy pressure indicates:
   creative power
   strong libido
   dominance
   enthusiasm
   involvement
   endurance
   resistance to exhaustion
   emotional strength
   deep commitments in love
   lasting memory (subconscious or conscious) of wrongs
   sensuousness
   desire for physical expression
   preference for dark or bright colors and rich foods
   unresolved anger

Extremely heavy pressure reveals poorly channeled energy as with a beginning writer, vanity, illness or secretiveness. If this pressure is combined with a slow writing it may indicate an inhibition without outlets, a depression and/or frustration.

Light pressure can be observed by thin lines, making no impression on the reverse side of the paper and very light color to the narrow inked lines.

Light pressure reveals:
    less intensity, vitality, and determination
    sensitive nature
    rapid forgiveness
    tenderness
    desire to avoid friction and commitment
    inclination to intuitiveness
    spirituality
    physical weakness
    preference for light pastel colors and light foods

Changing pressure announces:
    an inferiority complex
    moodiness
    unsteady will power
    inner conflicts
    emotional instability

Under most circumstances there is a slightly heavier pressure on the downstroke of the upper loops. If this is reversed and the pressure appears more pronounced on the upward stroke, a hostile environment may be indicated.

If pressure is absent on left descending upper zone strokes, a fear of the past is implied. If pressure is absent on right ascending upper zone strokes one may suspect fear of the future.

Sudden pressure changes such as club ending t bars or other club endings (blunt firm strokes) may reveal sudden emotional intensity or temper.

Pasty writing falls into two classes, both of which would use a large amount of ink, more than normal, to cover the same amount of paper by using thick strokes and filled in areas. The first class can indicate very positive traits. These strokes are heavy though clean cut, broad and firm, thick but never messy or blotchy.

This kind of pastyness indicates:
an aesthetic artistic nature
perceptiveness
unrestrained natural personality
pronounced pleasure in sense gratification
as feeling, touching, smelling, tasting.
warm, colorful, charming personality

The second class signifies unresolved and perhaps misunderstood sensual interests. These
strokes are messy and blotchy, filled in and
untidy. The handwriting is often very difficult
to read. It is frequently a very negative sign
which indicates:

    lack of self-discipline

    undependability

    maladjustment to life due often to a sexual
    basis

    possible erratic temperament

    concealing nature

STROKES

When analyzing a sample, practice the kinds of strokes the writer has made and then attempt to analyze your own feelings. Be aware of your own types of strokes and your feelings when you use one kind of stroke rather than another.

VI. STROKES

The three main kinds of strokes which will be discussed in this chapter are *Connecting, Beginning* and *Ending*. Information concerning connecting strokes will be listed first and of these strokes there are four main types. They are: Garland, Arcade, Angular and Thread. Very often individuals write with a combination of two or more of these and must be judged accordingly.

Garland:

avoids conflicts
has an adaptable personality
is kind and sympathetic
is outgoing
appears extroverted

Deep garland reveals a very receptive writer. This writer has a large cup to fill and will work at doing so by being receptive.

Shallow garland implies a somewhat receptive writer although this writer is more superficial and probably lacks restraint.

Arcade:

shields self, protective
builder, planner, structural sense
calculated amiability
concealing, covers up
places much importance on appearance
little importance on essence
lacks spontaneity

Angular:

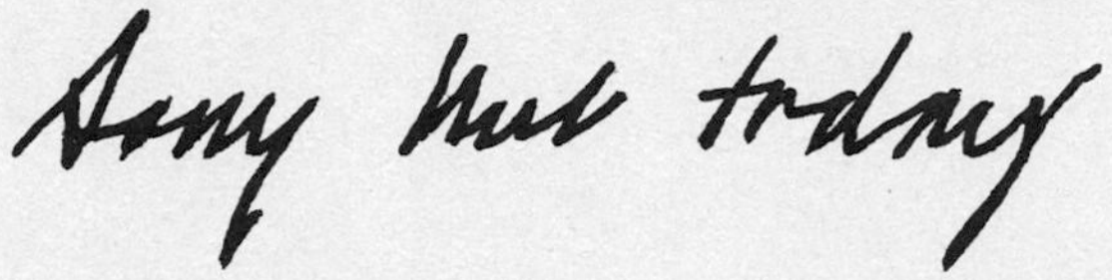

[handwritten zigzag angular strokes]

[handwritten cursive: Any but today]

refusal or inability to adapt
stubbornness, uncompromising nature
aggressiveness, competitiveness, stress
prejudice
idealism
initiative

Thread:

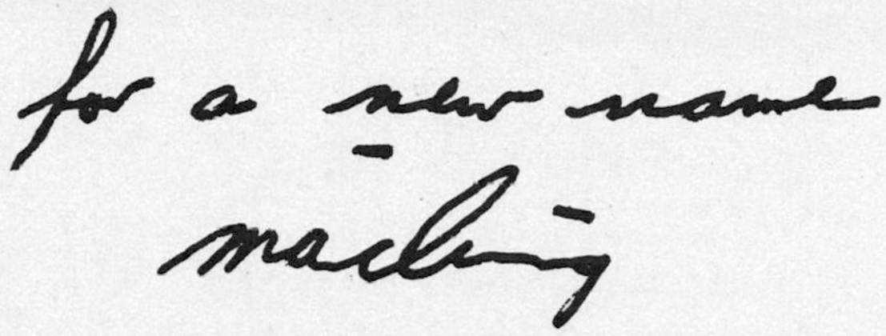

[handwritten straight line with arrow]

[handwritten cursive: for a new name]

[handwritten cursive: machine]

minimal resistance
insight, perceptiveness
adaptability
versatility
cunning and sneaky nature

In addition to the four types of connecting strokes the presence or absence of these strokes also holds important clues.

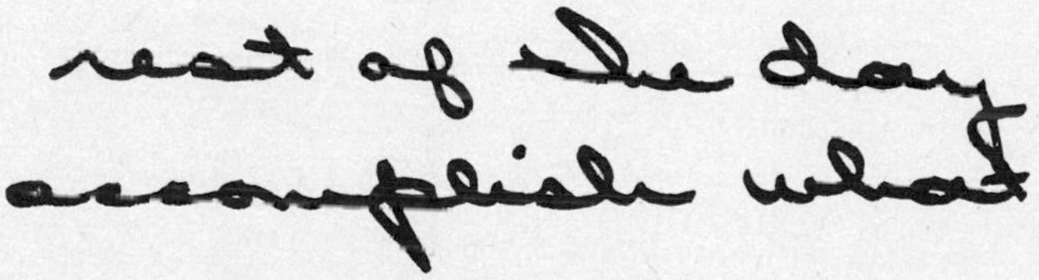

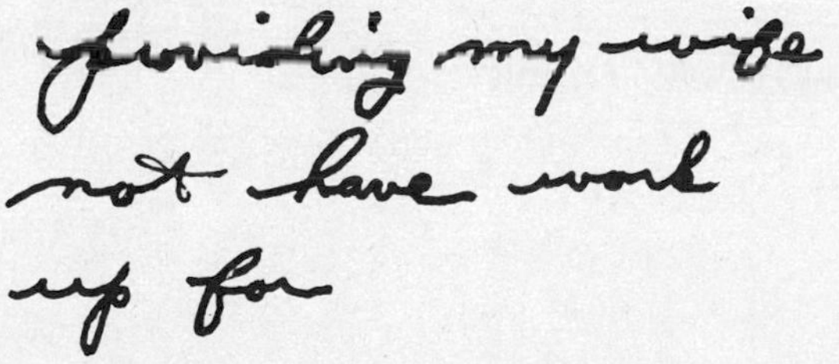

[handwritten cursive: rest of the day]

[handwritten cursive: accomplish what]

Connected writing of good form without breaks between letters within individual words announces:
   logical thinking
   a steady flow of thought
   adaptation to environment
   tenacity and persistence
   cooperative action
   lack of initiative

[handwritten cursive: providing my wife]

[handwritten cursive: not have work]

[handwritten cursive: up for]

wouldn't

sobbing continued

greeted by a

frantic call

appointment

Unconnected writing or breaks in the flow of ink between letters within words in writing of good form signifies:
    intuitive thought
    arrival at decisions quickly
    adaptation difficulties
    inventiveness
    independence
    unconforming nature
    willingness to stand alone
    self reliance
    individualistic
    unsociability

please send me

In poor form unconnected writing implies:
    unorganized thought
    irritability
    undisciplined nature
    possible physical defect
    uncooperativeness
    erratic nature without direction

Beginning strokes disclose the manner in which the writer grasps new situations or the calculated impression the writer makes; they announce the way the writer adjusts to a new job or assesses new situations; they show the writer's intentions.

kid to bed.

Fairly long curved beginning:
    not impulsive, needs time to prepare for activities
    obedient, comfortable with the past
    fussy about details
    needs to stand on own two feet

thought you interested.

Unbending beginning:
  tension from the past
  resentment against past
  less self assured and confident
  resistant to change

The longer the beginning stroke the more important the past remains.

tries hours morning

Unconnected first letter:
  The writer pauses before beginning anything
  observant (pause to look around)
  possibly dislikes decision (pause to avoid deciding)

this day

Unconnected last letter:
  Writer pauses after he is well into project but before he is really committed
  reconsiders decisions
  hesitant nature

what was

Long and below base line beginning stroke:
  subconscious drive to succeed
  impatient and aggressive in preparations

cthis

Curved right to left beginning:
  desire to own or save
  collector

two

Hooked beginning:
  jealousy acquisitive

M

Dark dot at beginning:
  "Skeleton in the closet" a hidden fact in past

Cathy

has been

knew but

thanks for being so thoughtful

Long underlining stroke:
   self-admiration
   self-importance

Beginning stroke starting in upper zone:
   idealistic
   religious awareness
   enterprise

Absent beginning:
   desire to begin without delay
   dislikes waste of time and energy
   objective
   practical
   intelligent
   not superficial

Ending strokes show social attitude. They show the writer as he is as opposed to the appearance given; the social manners or current behavior of the writer. These final strokes divulge the adaptability of the writer to the environment, the writing speed and attitudes based on past experience. They show his real nature and unconscious acts.

giggle

Long outward tending finals with blunt end:
   genuine giver
   generous

just

Upward tending final with tapered end:
   reluctant giver but giver
   perhaps expects reward or gain from giving

was

Very high reaching final:
    search for knowledge, perhaps occult
    interest

elled
– great

Blunt extended club-like ending:
    perhaps cruel and/or brutal
    firm and unyielding
    self comes first

glad

Blunt, unextended final:
    frankness and bluntness
    decisiveness concerning self

Patient

Sharp and below base line final:
    argumentative
    perhaps cruel
    perhaps obstinate

Chart

true sat

Final reaching back to left:
    introversion, self-protectiveness
    self-interest
    insecurity

him

Missing final:
    abrupt and unobliging, not a giver
    reserved and reticent
    honest, discriminating mind
    confidence in own resources

hands

up

be

Extended final:
    possessiveness
    caution

did

J

wg

ls gvrls

ban

maroon

Unfinished final:
    doesn't finish projects
    perhaps selfish

Coverstroke:
    screens thoughts and actions

Hook left and down:
    grasping
    greedy

Final pulling down and under:
    selfish
    concentrated self-interest above all else
    temper

Burst of pressure on final:
    temper
    unbearable emotions

Tapered whip final:
    temper

VII. SPACING

Spacing between words in writing is non deliberate just as spacing between words in speech usually is. The words follow after each other just as they do in speech. Transparencies No. 4 and 5 will probably be helpful in judging the evenness of the spacing. If the distance of the spacing is difficult to judge, the analyst might find helpful the expectation that the spaces take up roughly the same amount of room as a single letter.

Even spaces:
  ease with people
  reasonableness
  self-confidence
  good balance
  acceptance
  unadventuresomeness
  systematic carefulness

Uneven spaces:
  changeable social attitudes
  insecurity
  gullibility
  possible thought hesitation
  communication difficulty

Small spaces:
  extroversion
  talkativeness
  impulsiveness
  insecurity
  emotional spontaneity

Large spaces:
  critical and cautious nature

*this is a
known as a
spaces between*

introversion and pride
inhibition or shyness
isolation and objectivity
extravagance with self

Very large spaces:
  waste of paper and reader's time
  egotistical and inconsiderate
  marked isolation

Spacing between lines seems to be deliberately planned and signifies a picture of the organization of the writer's mind.

*much chance that he won't be
Brand, who is quickly getting the
he's speaking for a huge constit
are fed up with the anti-Nix
and the liberal establishment."*

Even line spacing:
  system and planning
  unadventuresome
  consistency

Wide line spacing:
  objectivity
  lonesomeness
  management ability
  mental agility
  good manners
  organization
  self-assurance
  lack of spontaneity

*eight o'clock and I
probably won't be
back 'til after
midnight*

Narrow line spacing:
  thriftiness
  hasty decision-making
  lack of reserve
  spontaneity
  frugality

we covered

It was quite

Very wide line spacing:
    possible separation of self from reality
    loneliness
    desire for non-involvement

thought of [?]ling mining /
trying to get land thro tax
g, little farming, sell blood in
ow successful they'll be & don't
al ramifications of [?]ling mining
& clipping of a newspaper article

Overlap of tangling, lower loops descending into line below:
    lack of inhibition
    preoccupation with instincts
    overinvolvement with activities

Afore the river
This morning

Upper zone ascending into line above:
    erotic fantasies which remain as daydreams
    without being demonstrated.

dry meat sufficien
scouts were ser
The coming of it
had been complet
The Mississippi t
Soux, descended
The water with
canoe suddenly I

Irregular line spacing:
    lack of will power
    disturbed reaction to environment
    changeable attitude about self

MARGINS

Margins are usually a more accurate measuring factor if the sample is on a full sheet (8 1/2 by 11 inches) of paper. Check your own margins, if possible, at different periods of your life and analyze your economic status, your desired position among your friends and the position which you really occupy.

VIII. MARGINS

Margins show the writer's degree of economy, consistency, tolerance, desire for esteem and urge for acceptance. The left, upper and lower margins are deliberately chosen while the right is only occasionally chosen. Well spaced margins signify an intelligent arrangement of time and space accompanied by favorable organization.

Wide upper margin
    formality
    reserve
    modesty
    esteem for reader
    withdrawal

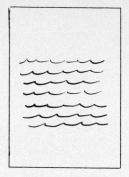

Wide lower margin
    superficiality
    aloofness
    idealism
    sexual or emotional trauma

Narrow upper margin
    informality
    directness
    lack of respect for reader

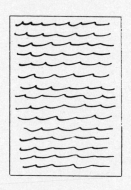

Narrow lower margin
    depression
    fatigue
    dreamer
    sensuousness
    materialistic

Left margins indicate the expectation of and desire for esteem; right margins show the distance the writer actually keeps between himself and others.

Wide left margin
  self respect
  high standards
  cultural background
  desired distance from others
  shyness

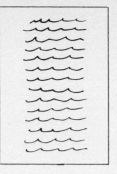

Wide right margin
  fear of future
  oversensitiveness
  unrealistic
  poor mixer, aloof
  wastefulness and extravagance
  fastidiousness

Extremely wide left
  flight from self
  very reserved
  snobbish
  unhappy childhood
  often divorced

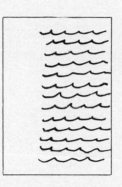

Narrow right
  desire for close relations
  deep urge for acceptance
  loquacity
  gregariousness
  joiner and mixer
  impulsiveness

Narrow left
  familiarity
  desire for popularity
  thriftiness or desire to receive due
  free and easy manner

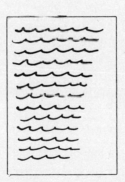

Widening right
  fear of others
  withdrawal

Widening left
    impatience
    haste
    enthusiasm
    impulsiveness
    lavishness
    waning thriftiness

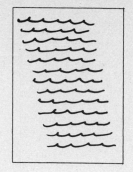

Narrowing right
    decreasing shyness

Narrowing left
    shyness
    unsociable
    progressive withdrawal
    depression
    unmanageable sense of thrift
    illness

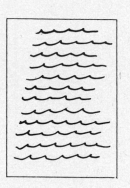

Irregular right
    unwise thriftiness
    love of travel
    ambivalent social attitude

Even left
    self discipline
    good manners

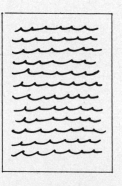

Even right
    intolerance
    conformity to set standards
    rigidity
    anxious and self conscious

Narrow, Absent on all sides
  stinginess
  acquisitiveness
  morbid curiosity
  tactlessness
  obtrusiveness
  unlimited sympathy

kindness
charity
fondness for luxury
hospitality

Wide all sides
  aesthetic
  lonely
  withdrawn

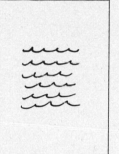

aloofness
spiritual independence
secrecy about self

Irregular all sides
  versatility
  tolerance
  disorganization

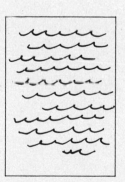

carelessness
inattentiveness

ALPHABET

The following pages contain some of the more widely used single letter traits arranged in alphabetical order. There are also some suggested forms for each individual letter which may or may not be comfortable and usable for you. Most of the suggested forms signify some of the traits which our society accepts as beneficial. This is the reason for their listing. It is not meant to be an indication that all individuals should make an attempt to use these forms.

You will often see different styles of letters which are not reproduced here but hopefully with this guide you will be able to assess the unknown through the known and arrive at a truthful conclusion.

Again it is most important that you not jump to a conclusion as a result of seeing a few clues which may indicate a personality trait but combine many different and repeated clues along with the overall picture to arrive at a final assessment.

a A a

Suggested Form

A's and O's are read for honesty, openess and talkativeness.

"Lincoln A"—protective, paternal

Large A made like small, only large in size—modest

Low cross bar—subordination

Sharp angles—hardness, resentment

Open at top—inaccurate and talkative

Narrow—shy

Large knot—pride in own and/or family achievement

Crossed at top—inexact, unconventional

Clean, closed—honest, reserved, introverted, secretive

Open—talkative

Knotted on left—not totally honest with others

Knotted on right—rationalizes, is not truthful to self

Double knot—dishonest to both self and others

Narrow knots—tells white lies

Open—talkative but not always truthful

Open on left—talks behind others backs

Covered—misrepresents self

Dangling hook—preoccupation with sex

Hook within—gross deceiver

Sharp angle—hidden greed

Open bottom—"Embezzeler's oval", lack of moral value

Encircled and/or enrolled—selfish, dishonest, cunning, evasive, untrustworthy

B B b

Suggested Form

B's are read for expressiveness and communication.

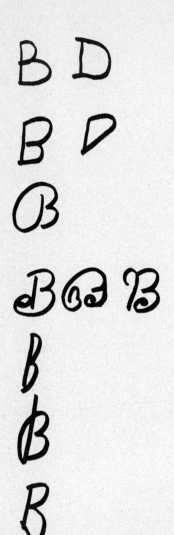

Wide bottom—gullible

Narrow bottom—skeptical

Wide beginning—bluffer

Encircled—egoist and/or concealing

Narrow—shy

Reaching beginning stroke—enterprising, thoughtful

Angular bottom—resentful, determined to have own way

Wide upper loop—expressive, imaginative

Narrow upper loop—reticence about self, unexpressive

Open bottom upstroke—credulous, gullible

Closed upstroke—good business sense, wary, shrewd

Short, full—humble individual who likes to talk about self

Tall, narrow—idealistic and/or religious aspect present

Without upper loop—taste and intelligence

Circled loop—imagination and poetic taste

Suggested Form

C's are read for formation and openness.
**The more closed or enrolled the person
is, the more like him his C appears.**

Encircled—concealing, perhaps hidden sex desires

Vertical loop—sense of responsibility toward others

Extended upper stroke—efficient worker, directness of character, spiritual or abstract awareness

Angular—quick, clever, realistic

Square—interest in building, mechanical

Complications—calculating mind

59

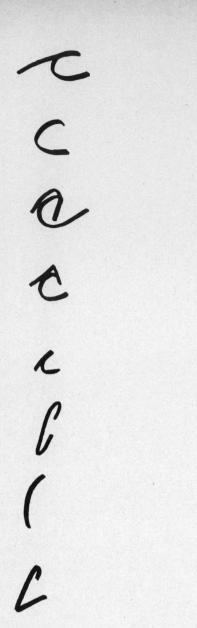

Beginning stroke—prop for writer

Plain and unadorned—idealistic and gracious, simple

Closed—writer shields self, protective

Pointed top—alert mind

As a small dotted I—quick witted, probably impatient

Narrow—shy and reserved

Arced—simple, straightforward, constructive

Angular bottom—resentful, insisting on own way

Suggested Form

D's are read for talkativeness, sensitivity concerning conduct and attire, and creativity.

Two parts—individualism, lack of adjustment

Broad arc, extended stroke—underlines own importance

Simplified—intelligence

Encircled—egoist, self interest

Open top—frankness, talkative

Closed top—reserved, keeps own counsel, secretive

Flying last stroke—flirtatious

Exceptionally wide—vanity and conceit

Open bottom—unreliable and dishonest

Open oval—talks about self

Closed oval—secretive about individual affairs

Low stem—humble, independent worker

High stem—idealist, proud, if retraced then dignified

Greek—aesthetic, poetic taste, flirtatious

Separated final stroke—"slow poke"

No upper loop, retraced—listener

Full upper loop—"thin skinned", very sensitive

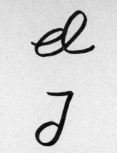

Knotted—diplomatic (adjusts truth to fit situation)

Left flag—protective, musical, creative

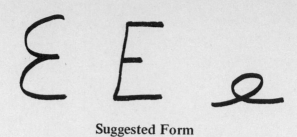

Suggested Form

Encircled—fussiness, primps, concealing, hoarder

Stroke cutting through from left—dress important

Angled—rigid, quick, clever, realistic

Underlining stroke—self admiration

Starting stroke touching loop—strain in mastering affairs

Left beginning arc—avarice

Concave arcs—good observer, simple approach to things

No loop—keen comprehension, quick thinker

Narrow loop—narrow minded

Broad loop—broadminded, willing to communicate, sometimes direct and outspoken

Greek—likes to read, refined taste, aesthetic

Final stroke going over original one—protective, selfish

Angle within letter—planner, calculating mind

Filled in with ink—sensual

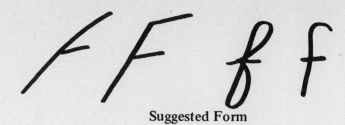

F's are read particularly for organization
and planning ability.

Fussy and ornate—vulgar, bad taste

Overhanging stroke—patronizing, protective

Narrow—shy

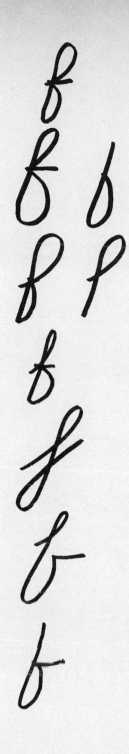

Balanced—well organized, managerial ability

Larger lower loop—physical orientation, active, energetic, poor organization in some area

Larger upper loop—mental orientation, doesn't place importance on physical aspects, poor organization in some area

Short full lower loop—food orientation, especially if heavy pressure is also present

Fluid double stroke—fluid thinker, original, smooth

Open lower loop—austere and unconcerned about image

Absent upper loop—forms own opinions

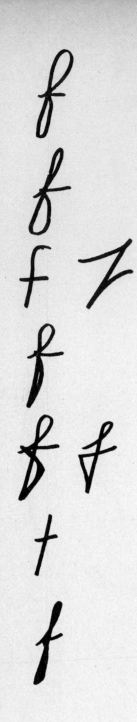

Full upper loop—articulateness

Narrow upper loop—perhaps narrow minded

Simple—artistic ability, intelligence, simple straight-forward approach

Angular point—resentful and uncompromising

Angular loop—strong reaction against interference

Cross form—concentration, fatalism

Ink filled—sensulality

Base Line Guide

TRANSPARENCY NO. 2

Slant Guide

TRANSPARENCY NO. 3

Pocket Guide

TRANSPARENCY NO. 1

Base Line Guide

TRANSPARENCY NO. 2

Slant Guide

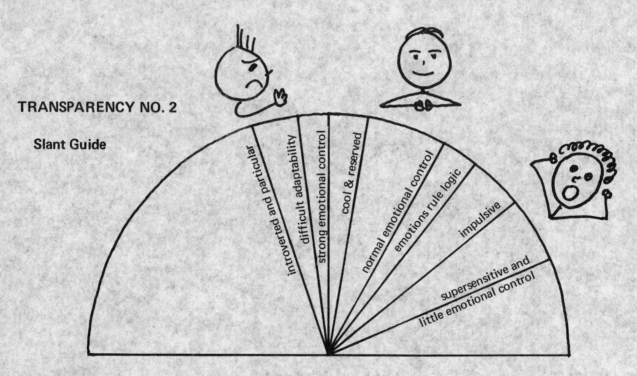

TRANSPARENCY NO. 3

Pocket Guide

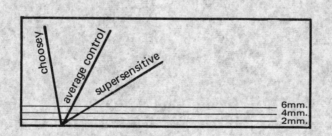

TRANSPARENCY NO. 1

3 X 3 mm. Graph

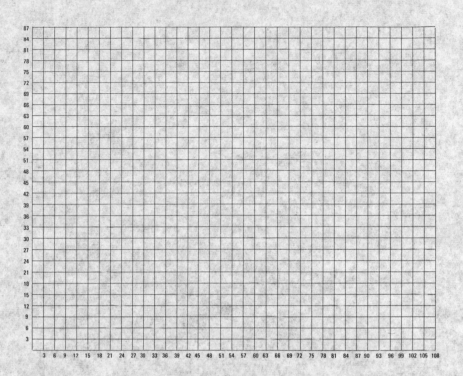

TRANSPARENCY NO. 2

2 X 2 mm. Graph

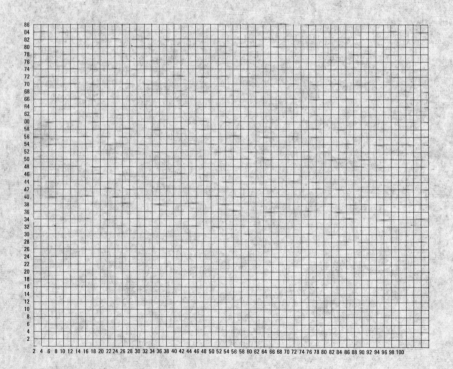

$$G \quad g \quad g \quad g \quad g$$

G's are read for attitudes toward and concerning sex, y's in relation to money and materialism.

Greek—literary talent, "a way with words", cultured, aesthetic

Arc left—not responsible

Large upper loop—"muddle head"

Simple—intelligent, straightforward

Blunt down stroke—supervisory ability, stands on own, stubborn, independent, determined

Long down stroke—many varied interests, restless, perhaps narrow minded

Small cramped loop—selective of friends, clannish

Large full loop—good imagination, dramatic ability, friendly, interested in physical activity, "on display", strong libido

Greek—literary ability, verbal fluency, fluid thinker

Open loop—unknowledgeable or unfulfilled concerning sex and/or money

Triangular loop—a domestic tyrant, or suffers from one

Knotted loop—abnormality in sex and/or money or maternal matters

Open 8 and narrow long loop—unusual sexual life

Left arc—sexual and/or material irresponsibility

Unfinished narrow loop—sexual weakness

Unfinished sharp point—sexual repression

Loop crossing below base line—frustration in sex or money

Left pulled loop—abnormal attachment to mother (childhood) and/or past

Last stroke swinging out and up—altrustic

Falling final stroke—despondency about sex and/or moncy

Upward swing to final stroke—initiative, optimism about sex and/or money

Omission of loop bottom—poor judgment. As in the y, the bottom of the money bag is missing.

Final stroke returns to left—vanity, selfishness, self concern

Very rounded loop—loyal

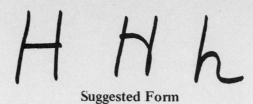

Suggested Form

"Houdini H"—strategist, knows how to get self out of situations

Simple—intelligent, firm ego

Narrow—shy

81

High round loop—spiritual awareness

Left downstroke—unwilling to compromise

Short upper loop—lack of thought or spiritual values

High narrow loop—opinionated, rigid spiritual upbringing

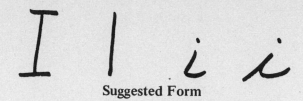

I's are read for detail importance and punctiliousness of the individual. The height of the dot may determine mental scope.

The capital I is very important, it is the ego image, the projection of self. It also indicates something of the writer's relationship with his parents.

Straight lines, printed—constructive, clear thinking, usually willing and capable, mechanical

Straight line—mature, stands alone, aware of own value, clear, concise

Upper loop more complete than lower—listens to mother

Lower loop more complete than upper—listens to father

Retraced upper loop—timid, repressed, doesn't talk of self

Large upper loop—talkative about self

Crossed out upper loop—rejects self, strict parents

Very small in comparison to other letters—low opinion of self

Not finished nor started well—doesn't like people, poorly formed ego

Left leaning—introvert, self-critic, particularly if rest of writing is right slanted

Right slanted—extrovert, needs and likes people

Far right slanted—always considers self first

"Rocking chair"—observes but doesn't involve self, also accepting of father even if he doesn't measure up to standards

Knot on second loop—forceful, talks about unpleasantness with father

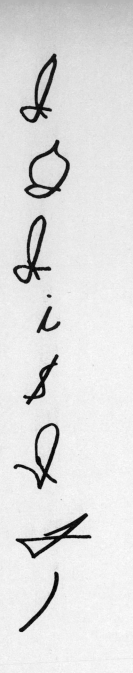

Pointed upper loop—keen mind

"Candle flame"—penetrating, consuming

Tall—proud and idealistic

Small letter—writer feels worthless in eyes of others

Dollar sign—parents represent money

Left arc—irresponsible

Angular—resentment, critical of self, hostile

Curve—takes easy way out, not involved

i ⸱ High dot—good imagination, dreamer

i High, flying dot—curiosity seeker, impatience and enthusiam

i Round, justly placed dot—detail conscious, accurate, precise, concentration

i Absence of dot—careless, absent minded

i Circle—frustrated, attention demanding, imaginative, artistic, individualist, dislikes routine work, likes fads, loyal to ideas and standards

i Leftfaced dot—neurotic

i Right faced dot—observant

i Flying V—sarcastic

v Tent dot—critical

i   Right faced angle dot—fault finder, critical, appraises and evaluates people

i   Left placed dot—dislikes decisions, procrastinates

i   Dash to right—enthusiastic, perhaps irritable

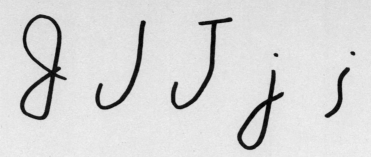

Suggested Form

J's are read like the lower loops on G's
and Y's. Lower case J's are read like the
I dot and have combined meanings.

K K K kk

Suggested Form

Simple—mechanical, intelligent

Second stroke higher—ambition

Second stroke longer—bluntness, defensive

Knot left of vertical bar—exotic past experiences and is still thinking of them

Point through bar—resents opposite sex

"Loving K", knot wrapped around bar—likes sex and people

Distant second stroke—cool and distant, afraid of sex

Second stroke just touching bar—teaser

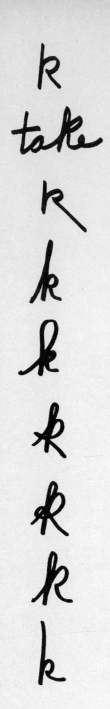

Rounded second stroke—yields, gives in, broadminded in argument

High second stroke—rebel, resents authority, protests, defends self and others

Second stroke leaning—stubborn

Narrow loop—opinionated

Inflated loop—inflated philosophical imagination

Middle stroke passes through bar—concerned with image

Middle stroke looped through bar—concerned with image and resents it

Middle stroke doesn't reach bar—unconcerned with image

Extended upper stroke—enterprise

93

L L $\mathcal{L}$ $\mathcal{l}$

Suggested Form

Simple—cultured, artistic taste

Missing lower loop—reserved, secretive

Missing upper loop—positiveness, reserved, materialistic

Larger base loop—self importance, vain

Larger upper loop—generous

Enrolled—concealing, vulgar

Beginning grasping arc—greedy, loves money

Sharp point—penetrating mind

Broad loop—broadminded, imaginative, philosophical

Narrow loop—opinionated, philosophical, reserved

Straight—quick mind, sensible, intuitive

Tall—likes to make speeches and organize

MMNNmn

Curved beginning—good natured, sense of humor

Straight horizontal begininning—dry humor

Incurve—family pride, may hide family secret, sensitive, may dislike self

Block—aesthetic, prefers essential only

Vertical beginning loop "money bag"—love of responsibility, likes to handle money

Open bag—desires responsibility but unable to handle

Second stroke high—dependent on private rather than public opinion, social ambition

Third stroke high—looks up to others, immature, envious, self-conscious; fear of being watched or judged; need to be in a position of authority in order to feel adequate

Tapering—diplomatic, condescending

Center downstroke short—tactless

Squeezed—shrewd, suspicious, sizes people up

Second stroke peaked—rude

"Temper tic", sharp beginning stroke—temper and gambler but "above board gambler"

Sharp beginnning stroke—"card shark", "underhanded"

Lower loops present— worry about self

Square or small horizontal beginning loop—jealous

These three descriptive terms are explained in the chapter on strokes.

Garland

Arcade

Angular

Rounded—gentle, works with hands, molds, creates, logical, accumulative, analytical and deliberate thinker

Peaked—works with mind, bright thinker, fast comprehension, sifts facts

Final stroke pointed—temper, critical fault finder

Four loops—accident prone, under mental strain

Upper strokes looped—clairvoyance

Lower strokes looped—worries about others

First stroke looped—attempts to cover up worrying

Third hump unfinished—dishonesty

Tall peaked first stroke—pride

Last stroke left tending—repression, shrewdness

Left arc—acquisitive

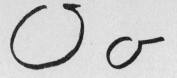

Suggested Form

Upper and lower case O's are read the
same as upper and lower case A's.

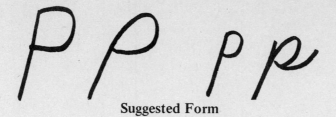

Suggested Form

P's show amount of physical activity.

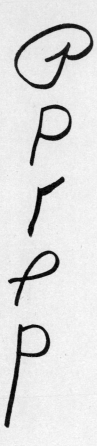

Inflated—infatuation of ego, the more inflated the more vulnerable the writer, imaginative

Simple—love for the beautiful, good taste, intelligence

Original—brilliant mind, creative

Terminal crossing over bar—reserved, discreet

Tall—pride and vanity

Large loop—physical minded, goes where the action is, dancer, likes sports

Retraced lower loop—good physical stamina and endurance, participant in sports (hiking, etc.)

Short upper stem—writer unwilling to go out of the way, expects pay for favors

High upper stem—charitable, expands energies without expecting remuneration

Open bag—talks to animals or self, relaxed spending

First stroke looped—argumentative, imaginative

First stroke small loop—quarrelsome

First stroke peaked—peaceful nature, sensitive to noise

Suggested Form

Q's are read for ovals and lower loops.

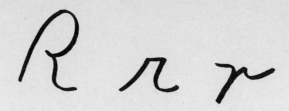

Suggested Form

R's are read for taste and pride, for music and ability with hands.

Simple—reader, cultured, intelligent

Second stroke shorter—ambitious

First stroke reaching—enterprising

"Table top"—broadminded about religion, works with hands, skill with tools

"Needle top"—perceptive, observant, sharp mind

"Lazy R"—deliberate, dull, unobservant

First stroke higher—curious, visual acuity, critical and particular

"Parochial R"—suppressed thinking, rule follower, probably went to a private school

Printed—able to write thoughts without difficulty

Double peaks—finger dexterity in both hands

Knot on first stroke —sings to self

Suggested Form

Simple—culture, taste; Printed—mechanical, constructive ability

Treble clef—likes music, may be musical if rhythm present

Left arc—avoids responsibilities

"Lazy S"—easy going, mentally lazy

Upper peak—stubborn, investigative

Rounded top—yielding, gives in

Closed loop—secretive

Enrolled—shrewdness, greed

Lower loop—tenacity

Undulating—artistic taste

Small capital—writer stands on ceremony, does things "according to Hoyle"

Loop on top of main body—imagination in addition to the above

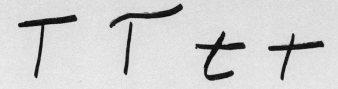

Suggested Form

Extended bar—protective

Fussy, ornate—bad taste

Left tending strokes—attachments to past

Stems

Retraced stem—repressed nature and unexpressive

Looped stem—talkative and articulate, sensitive about work, bothered by criticism; does not do as others do just because he must conform

Inflexible beginning stroke—resentful and stubborn

Stubbornness, deceptiveness; evasive

Stem Height reflects Idealism

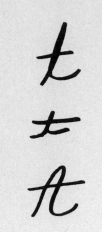

High stem—idealistic thinker, high goals

Short stem—timid, works alone and often called independent worker, doesn't take chances

Spread out stem—slow worker, indolent

Bar pressure shows will power

Light pressure—doesn't compete, less will power and vitality, sensitive

Beginning heavy but bar feathers out—indecisive, gives up

Heavy pressure—firm, tendency to always be right, good will power

Bar height indicates goals

Bar above stem—daydreamer, shows his annoyance

High bar—high goals, dynamic, idealistic, pride and ability, ambitious, long range planner

Well balanced cross—precise, organized, self controlled, reachable goals

Low bar—low goals, obedience, patience, inferiority complex, humble, self doubter

Length of crossing indicates control

Long and sharp—sarcastic, cruel at times

Long—enthusiastic

Long continuing over other letters to cross another T—mental gymnast, plans actions and efforts

Short—underachiever, lack of control or desire for control

Other bars

Bowed crossing—attempts at self control, inhibition of instinct

Left bowed crossing—attempts to control procrastination

Shallow crossing—sense of humor, shallow thinking, easy going, easily influenced

"Star T"—sense of responsibility, sensible

Star with tie—sense of responsibility but resents it, persistent, tenacious

Whip ending—indomitable, untamable, temper

Crossing back—self pity, egotism, perhaps jealousy, possible withdrawal to past

Cross to left—dislikes making decisions, puts off doing things

Cross to right—fast thinker, impulsive, perhaps easily irritated and on occasion, tactless

Absent bar—absent minded in work, careless or preoccupied and unattentive to details

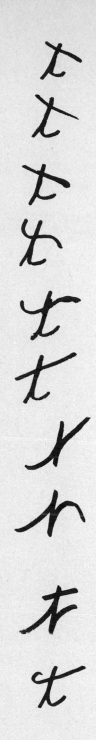

Bar with blunt downstroke—dominates and influences, determined

Bar with tapered downstroke—bossy, domineering

Heavy blunt club downstroke—destructive, brutal, aggressive, determined

Undulating downstroke—prodigious obstinacy

Undulating bar—mimic, fun loving, wishy washy, frivolous, humorous

Up slanted bar—optimistic; if heavy, then also aggressive

Last stroke directed up and out—easy going, initiative, fluency, speed, unrestrictive

Last stroke directed down—initiative not completed because of pessimistic attitude

Last stroke directed out but stem also crossed—easygoing, but can suddenly become determined and willful, unpredictable

Hook on the left of bar—acquisitive, needs to get work out of the way

Hook on the right of bar—hanger-on, bulldog, greedy

Changing bars—unstable in goals, control and will power, but may be versatile

U U u

Suggested Form

U's may also be read as an inverted N.

𝓊

U

Undulating beginning stroke—sense of humor

Simple—good mind, straightforward in approach

Angular—resistant

Retraced—repressed, unexpressive

Arcade—protective, fearful, appearances important

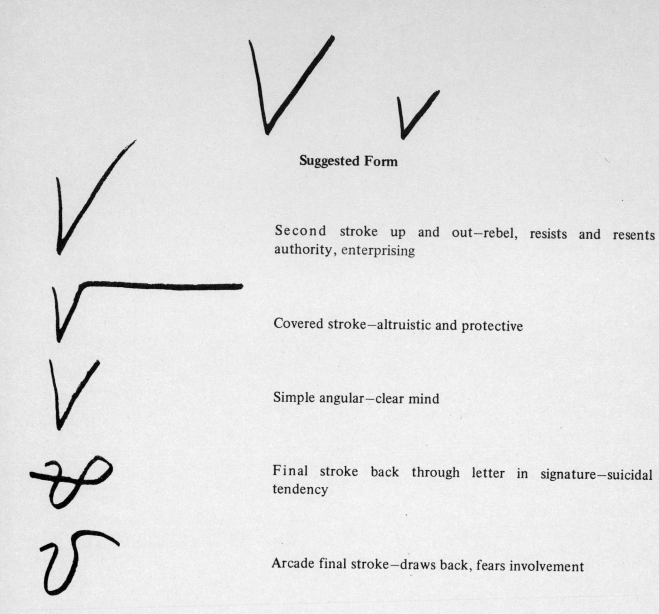

Suggested Form

Second stroke up and out—rebel, resists and resents authority, enterprising

Covered stroke—altruistic and protective

Simple angular—clear mind

Final stroke back through letter in signature—suicidal tendency

Arcade final stroke—draws back, fears involvement

125

W W w w

Suggested Form

Curved and sharp strokes—likes beautiful things

Vertical beginning—likes responsibility

Wavy beginning stroke—sense of humor

Tie on last stroke—poetic taste

Angular—analytical

Curved in on itself—lives in past, fearful of future

Simple—good mind, clear thinker

Suggested Form

Precise cross—precision, perhaps defensive

Blunt club stroke to left—stabs toward or at past, temper

Curve and line—work toward future

Separate lines—talkative, difficulty in adapting

High right strokes—enterprise and ambition

Y Y Y Y Y

Suggested Form

Y's are read as G's.

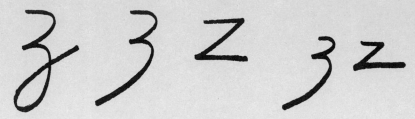

Suggested Form

Z's are read for loops and legibility.

Underlining stroke—self admiration

Simple—clear, keen mind, perhaps constructive

Curved—easy going

Downstroke unfinished—depression

X. CONCLUSION

As previously mentioned, each trait discussed in this book is only one clue and must be combined with other clues to give the analyst a true picture of the writer's personality.

The blank pages and spaces in this book will help the reader form his own textbook. As he becomes aware of other traits and factors and adds them in the appropriate areas, a complete personal reference will emerge, that is more valuable than hundreds of purchased textbooks.

There follows a list of recommended books for further study and several resources for information concerning analyses, specialty fields, instruction and graphological organizations.

Ruth Gardner
Llewellyn Publications
Box 3383
St. Paul, Minnesota 55165

Prince Bokovoy, Jr.
260 Xerxes North
Minneapolis, Minnesota 55405

Alex Sjoberg
P.O. Box 745
Downsview
Ontario, Canada

Charlie Cole
Box 423
Santa Clara, California

Leslie King
Handwriting Consultants of Utah
Box 364
Bountiful, Utah

HAM
Handwriting Analysts of Minnesota
341 Dayton Avenue
St. Paul, Minnesota

BIBLIOGRAPHY

Bunker, M. N. *Handwriting Analysis.* Chicago: Nelson-Hall Company.

de Sainte Colombe. *Grapho-Therapeutics.* Hollywood California: Laurida.

Holder, Robert. *You Can Analyze Handwriting.* Hollywood, California: Wilshire 1965.

Jacoby, H. J. *Analysis of Handwriting.* London: Allen and Unwin.

Leibel, Charlotte B. *Change Your Handwriting—Change Your Life.*

Martin, Kevin. *What Your Handwriting Reveals.* New York: Meredith.

Mendel, Alfred. *Personality in Handwriting.* New York: Stephen Daye.

Myer, Oscar N. *Language of Handwriting.*

Olyanova, Nadya. *Psychology of Handwriting.* Hollywood, California: Wilshire.

Roman, Dr. Klara. *Handwriting: Key to Personality.* New York: Noonday.

Rosen, Billie. *The Science of Handwriting Analysis.* New York: Bonanza.

Saudek, R. *Experiments with Handwriting.* London: Allen and Unwin.

Singer, Eric. *A Manual of Graphology.* London: Duckworth and Company.

Smith, Hanna. *Between the Lines.*